D0867694

The

S *of* SONG OLOMON

A study of Love, Sex, Marriage and Romance

by

Tommy Nelson

HUDSON
PRODUCTIONS

DALLAS, TEXAS

www.songofsolomon.com

1st Edition published 1995, 2nd Edition published 1999
by Hudson Productions
7160 N. Dallas Parkway, Suite 360
Plano, Texas 75024

Editor in Chief:
    Carrie Hudson
    Doug Hudson

All Scripture quotations are taken from
the Ryrie Study Bible, 1978 Edition
The New American Standard Translation
Moody Press, Chicago

Printed in the United States of America

Additional Tommy Nelson Resources

Ideal for personal or group Bible study:

The Song of Solomon: A Study of Love, Sex, Marriage and Romance
6-cassette tape or 6-CD Audio Series.
4-VHS tape or 4-DVD Video Series.
86-page Study Guide.

The Song of Solomon for Students
2-cassette VHS Videotape Series.
68-page Study Guide.
Facilitator's Guide.

The Big Picture: Understanding the Story of the Bible
256-page softcover book by Tommy Nelson
that explains the biblical narrative in an easy-to-read format.

Other resources:

The Book of Romance,
220-page hardcover book based on the series,
The Song of Solomon.

The Problem of Life with God,
212-page hardcover book based on the series,
Ecclesiastes.

My Beloved:
Music and Thoughts from The Song of Solomon
10-song CD by Michael Armstrong.

Conference:

The Song of Solomon Conference, a dynamic, humorous and candid seminar
on love, sex, marriage and romance, featuring Tommy Nelson.

Contact us at 1.800.729.0815 or www.songofsolomon.com
or write to Hudson Productions,
7160 N. Dallas Parkway, Suite 360, Plano, Texas 75024

Acknowledgements

This project has been a living example of God's hand working through His people. There have been many people and institutions which have made this project possible. We would like to thank the following:

*The thousands of people who have attended this study
and whose lives have been changed.*

Prestonwood Baptist Church, for its support in all areas.

Denton Bible Church and elders for its support and encouragement.

Dal Shealy, Bill Krisher and the entire Fellowship of Christian Athletes

Frank Gates

Billy Wilson

Steve Smith

Greg Gorman

Brian Maxwell Smith

There have been many more who helped this project become a reality, and to all of you, we thank you.

God gets all the glory!

Contents

Hudson Productions

Doug Hudson, president of Hudson Productions, started METRO Bible study at Prestonwood Baptist Church in 1992, where he served as Minister to Single Adults from 1990-98. Doug and his wife, Carrie, have three children: K.K., born in June 1996, Macy, born in March 1999, and Mac, born in December 2001.

In 1993, Doug contacted Tommy Nelson, senior pastor of Denton Bible Church and invited him to teach a four-week series at METRO (now attended by more than 3,000 people weekly). In January 1994, Tommy accepted the invitation to teach METRO full-time, and his first series was the Song of Solomon. Attendance at METRO increased from 600 to more than 2,000 people during the six-week series. In May 1995, he repeated the series—and attendance ballooned from 1,200 to more than 4,000. Based on this response, the audio and video series—as well as this study guide—were created.

The Song of Solomon material changed the lives of Doug and Carrie. The first time they heard the series, their relationship was about one month old. God allowed them to hear His best for a romantic relationship through his messenger, Tommy Nelson. "It gave us the greatest foundation," Doug says. "God allowed us to start our marriage off on the right foot. The study of the Song of Solomon works!"

In February 1997, FamilyLife Ministries aired The Song of Solomon material for six days. The response was unprecedented in the four years of their broadcast. Two years later, the material again was aired and had similar results.

After much prayer, Doug resigned from Prestonwood Baptist Church to launch Hudson Productions. This decision was made after seeing God's blessing on the Song of Solomon material and recognizing the effectiveness of this message throughout the world at a grass-roots level.

Hudson Productions exists to create tools and resources to encourage individuals and churches. Our fourfold goal is: 1) To edify the Body of Christ; 2) To equip churches with quality and effective resources; 3) To equip existing Christians with quality and effective resources; and 4) To develop resources that help churches and ministries reach individuals searching for the Truth.

Ultimately, our goal is to fulfill the Great Commission.

Introduction

The Song of Solomon has changed our lives. The first time we heard the series our relationship was about a month old. God allowed us to hear His best for a romantic relationship through his messenger Tommy. It gave us the greatest foundation. Eighteen months later Tommy did the series again, and we had been married for one month. God allowed us to then start our marriage off on the right foot. The study of The Song of Solomon works!

The purpose of the study guide is to enhance the audio and video series. It is not designed to replace them. This guide is made for either individuals or groups to listen, watch, make notes and have discussion time.

Romantic relationships obviously affect all of us. We would not be here if it was not for a romantic relationship between our mothers and fathers. For too long we have waited for somebody to stand up and teach the truth about this God-given desire for the opposite sex and the holy institution of marriage. Tommy Nelson has been teaching this material for the past ten years and has seen how the truth of God's Word is no less true in dealing with our passion.

Our goal for this material is significant, because we believe—along with thousands of others—that this material is significant. The goal is to allow everyone in the United States the opportunity to hear this material in some form. This is a God-sized goal, and we are praying for a revival by God through this incredible part of our lives—our romantic lives. Please pray and work with us to accomplish this worthy goal.

Now, enjoy the study. We know your life and your family's life will be richly blessed by God.

For His Work,

Doug and Carrie Hudson

How to Use This Study Guide at a Conference

At the conference, Tommy teaches a total of six sessions—three on Friday evening and three on Saturday. The Study Guide consists of 12 chapters, and Tommy covers two chapters per session at the conference. For example: during the first session Friday night, he will cover chapters 1-2. The Study Guide contains the biblical text, so when Tommy finishes teaching the text, proceed to the next chapter. Note that during the conference, Tommy will not cover every question printed in the study guide.

The Study Guide contains more information than you will receive at the conference, but we want you to have the entire material so that you can continue an in-depth personal study at home. The Study Guide also is designed for use with the Audio and Video Series. See below.

How to Use This Study Guide in a Bible Study

The Study Guide contains 12 chapters that follow directly with the Audio and Video Series. We suggest that each individual have a Study Guide, which will enable them to take notes and write key thoughts in the Study Guide. The Audio and Video Series contains 12 thirty-minute sessions.

For a 12-week study, we suggest showing one thirty-minute session from the Audio or Video Series per meeting, then lead group discussions and go through key Text and Application Questions.

For a six-week study, show two thirty-minute sessions from the Audio or Video Series per meeting, then lead group discussions and go through key Text and Application Questions.

Foreword

Love, sex, marriage and romance can serve as the ultimate Jekyll and Hyde of life. On one hand, they give us great joy and satisfy the deepest desires and needs, but such desires can also turn on us and plunge our lives into the deepest of pain. Has God given us these desires, drives and needs, and yet failed to give us any guidance through what can be such treacherous ground? I think not. He has given us the Song of Solomon. As you study this book with me, may you be blessed, enlightened and directed by the good Word of God, the Great Designer of life and all of its delights and joys.

Tommy Nelson

Author Information

Since 1977, Tommy Nelson has been the Pastor of Denton Bible Church, located in Denton, Texas. He has been featured on Focus On The Family, FamilyLife Today, Josh McDowell, For Faith and Family, and other national broadcasts. Tommy graduated from the University of North Texas with a Bachelor's Degree in Education. He then attended Dallas Theological Seminary in Dallas, Texas, where he received the Master of Arts in Biblical Studies degree. In addition to the Song of Solomon materials, he is the author of two books: *The Book of Romance* and *The Big Picture: Understanding the Story of the Bible*. Tommy has been married to Teresa Nelson for more than 25 years. He is the father of two adult sons, Benjamin and John.

SESSION ONE
The Art of Attraction

INTRODUCTION

The Art of Attraction is the beginning of romance. There are two questions each person should ask: what kind of person am I attracted to? and what kind of person is attracted to me? Many people continue to date the same kind of person and continue to have the same problems in dating relationships. Attraction is about becoming the person God wants you to be and allowing God to bring to you the kind of person He knows is best for you. This lesson is the foundation for the entire study. To whom a person is attracted shows a great deal about the character and personality of him/her. To whom we are attracted—and therefore date—is ultimately going to be a person we will marry.

SCRIPTURE:

Song of Solomon chapter 1, verses 1-7

1   *1 The Song of Songs, which is Solomon's.*
2 "May he kiss me with the kisses of his mouth!
For your love is better than wine."
3 "Your oils have a pleasing fragrance,
Your name is like purified oil;
Therefore the maidens love you."
4 "Draw me after you and let us run together!
The king has brought me into his chambers.
We will rejoice in you and be glad;
We will extol your love more than wine.
Rightly do they love you."
5 "I am black but lovely,
O daughters of Jerusalem,
Like the tents of Kedar,
Like the curtains of Solomon."
6 "Do not stare at me because I am swarthy,
For the sun has burned me.

My mother's sons were angry with me;
They made me caretaker of the vineyards,
But I have not taken care of my own vineyard."
7 "Tell me, O you whom my soul loves,
Where do you pasture your flock,
Where do you make it lie down at noon?
For why should I be like one who veils herself
Beside the flocks of your companions?"

[handwritten: Sees in The light]

[handwritten: not]

[handwritten: Like The whore]

 # TEXT NOTES

[handwritten: Looks are cancelled out by character]

[handwritten: The Rouge man vs The Man-eater]

TEXT QUESTIONS

1) There are three sections to the Old Testament:
   1) Historic, including what books?

   2) Poetic, including what books?

   3) Prophetic, including what books?

2) What are two of the qualities Abraham looked for in a wife?

3) Song of Solomon 1:3b, "Your name is like purified oil."
   What does this Scripture mean?

4) Song of Solomon 1:6b, "My mother's sons were angry with me;
   They made me caretaker of the vineyards..." What does this verse mean?

5) Song of Solomon 1:7b, "For why should I be like the one who veils herself
   beside the flocks of your companions?" How does Tommy interpret this?

 ## APPLICATION QUESTIONS

1) How is God sovereign over your love and passion?

2) Why does Tommy say "If he will not obey God as a single, he will break your
   heart as a married man."

3) Do you find yourself pressing your partner morally? Why?
   Is your partner pressing you morally? Why?

4) How does God want you to deal with your desire/passion?

5) What differences are there in the way this couple attracts verses the way the world tells us?

6) "Charm is deceitful and beauty is in vain." Why do we look to ourselves and the world (magazines, movies, etc.) rather than to the Word of God for answers to our relationship questions?

7) How much time do you spend worrying about your looks vs. your character? Why?

8) What is meant by "it is better to be lonely and single than lonely and married?"

9) How do you allow Christ to fulfill the loneliness that can come with being single?

10) Prioritize the qualities you are looking for in a mate:
    1)
    2)
    3)
    4)
    5)

11) Prioritize the qualities you are looking for in a friend:

      1)

      2)

      3)

      4)

      5)

12) How can you remain accountable to these priorities? Be specific.

13) What qualities do you have to offer to a mate?

14) What qualities do you have to offer to a friend?

15) Song of Solomon 1:3b, "Your name is like purified oil." A man's name is his character/integrity. Are people attracted to the value of your name? Why? Why not?

16) What do you think God would say about your character?

FOCUS POINT

Tommy shares perhaps one of the greatest illustrations about attraction that has ever been told. A person looking for a mate is like running on a track. The track is a personal relationship with Jesus Christ. The goal of the race is to become more like Christ. As we run we will see others running the race as well. When a person is running, he will see another running the same pace they are. After awhile, one might say, "hey, let's run a lap or two together and see what it is like." In time, the man will say at some point, "We are both running the same race, the race for Christ. Why don't we run the race together?" Finding a mate is not a race unto itself. It is something that naturally happens when we run God's race.

17) What do you know about the character of God? Be specific.

18) What do you think Tommy means when he says, "Sin is always ugly in the dark"?

19) What sin do you need to bring out of the dark?

 ## KEY QUESTIONS

Are you running in the Race for God?

    How?

    Is your mate?

    Are your friends?

    Do you know someone who isn't?

    What can you do to help others run the race?

What was the most meaningful point you heard today? Why?

In light of what you have viewed today, how would you like to become more like this couple?

KEY THOUGHT

"All that glitters is not gold; All that is gold does not necessarily glitter."

MEMORY VERSE

Men: Proverbs 31:30
"Charm is deceitful and beauty is vain, But a woman who fears the Lord, she shall be praised."

Women: Proverbs 19:22
"What is desirable in a man is his kindness, And it is better to be a poor man than a liar."

PRAYER REQUESTS

SESSION TWO
The Art of Dating

INTRODUCTION

The Art of Dating begins with time. Once a person is attracted to someone, the dating process begins. The best kind of dating is time spent getting to know one another. Too many people move too quickly in the dating process. The goal of a great date is to build respect for one another. A person cannot respect someone if they do not know them. They cannot get to know them unless they spend time together. A great date is not centered around entertainment alone, but around quality time in a safe environment. How does a person know if they like a person if they don't invest the time to learn who they are? Dating is a process of time, cultivation, and restraint.

SCRIPTURE:
Song of Solomon chapter 1, verses 8-17; chapter 2, verses 1-7

1 8 *"If you yourself do not know,*
Most beautiful among women,
Go forth on the trail of the flock,
And pasture your young goats
By the tents of the shepherds."
9 "To me, my darling, you are like
My mare among the chariots of Pharaoh."
10 "Your cheeks are lovely with ornaments,
Your neck with strings of beads."
11 "We will make for you ornaments of gold
With beads of silver."
12 "While the king was at his table,
My perfume gave forth its fragrance."
13 "My beloved is to me a pouch of myrrh
Which lies all night between my breasts."
14 "My beloved is to me a cluster of henna blossoms
In the vineyards of Engedi."

15 "How beautiful you are, my darling
How beautiful you are!
Your eyes are like doves."
16 "How handsome you are, my beloved,
And so pleasant!
Indeed, our couch is luxuriant!"
17 "The beams of our houses are cedars,
Our rafters, cypresses.

2 *1 "I am the rose of Sharon,*
The lily of the valleys."
2 "Like a lily among the thorns,
So is my darling among the maidens."
3 "Like an apple tree among the trees of the forest,
So is my beloved among the young men.
In his shade I took great delight and sat down,
And his fruit was sweet to my taste."
4 "He has brought me to his banquet hall,
And his banner over me is love."
5 "Sustain me with raisin cakes,
Refresh me with apples,
Because I am lovesick."
6 "Let his left hand be under my head
And his right hand embrace me."
7 "I adjure you, O daughters of Jerusalem,
By the gazelles or by the hinds of the field,
That you will not arouse or awaken my love,
Until she pleases."

 # TEXT NOTES

TEXT QUESTIONS

1) Romans 13:14, "...make no provisions for the_____ in regard to its_____."

2) I Peter 3:4, "...but let it be the hidden person of the heart, with the imperishable quality of a gentle and quiet spirit, which is precious in the sight of God." What does it mean to be this kind of a woman? Give examples.

3) Song of Solomon 2:4, "...and his banner over me is love."
According to Tommy, what does this mean?

4) Song of Solomon 2:6, "Let his left hand be under my head and his right hand embrace me." What does this portray?

5) Song of Solomon 2:7b, "...that you will not arouse or awaken my love, until she pleases." What does this mean?

APPLICATION QUESTIONS

1) According to Tommy, the greatest sex organ on a woman is her mind. Why?

2) How do the "three things needed in a relationship" apply to your relationship?
  *time:

  *cultivation:

  *restraint:

3) How are you cultivating your relationship with God?

4) How do you cultivate respect with your mate?

THE TEN STEPS OF SEXUAL GRADATION:

1-hand to hand
2-hand to shoulder
3-hand to waist
4-face to face
5-hand to head
6-body to body (hug)
7-mouth to face
8-mouth to mouth
9-hand to body
10-body to body

5) How important is the physical to you in light of its temporary nature?

6) According to Tommy, "passion is the worst foundation for a marriage." Why?

7) Why is immorality compared to the law of diminishing return?

8) Would you want the person you are with today to raise your children and teach them his/her character?

9) When you conflict, do you try to prove your point or deepen the relationship?

   Why?

10) "Satan will tell your wife or girlfriend she is special if you won't." How can you prevent this from happening in your relationship?

11) Are you looking/is your partner looking outside the relationship for a need the partner should be fulfilling? Why?

12) Is your partner a banner to you? Why? Why not?

13) "Tenderness is the greatest need of a woman."
Men: What are you doing to cultivate tenderness in your partner's life?

14) What does it mean to "pimp tenderness?"

15) "Respect is the greatest need of a man."
Women: What are you doing to cultivate respect in your partner's life?

 KEY QUESTIONS

What was the most meaningful point you heard today? Why?

In light of what you have viewed today, how would you like to become more like this couple?

 KEY THOUGHT

"Marry your best friend."

 MEMORY VERSE

Song of Solomon 3:5b
"...that you will not arouse or awaken love, until it pleases."

 PRAYER REQUESTS

SESSION THREE
The Art of Courtship, Part I

INTRODUCTION

The Art of Courtship is the beginning of sacrifice and commitment between two people. Dating could be described as "kicking tires" or "browsing in a store." Courtship is when the two people know the other is special and want to know more about them. Courtship is a risk between two people.

SCRIPTURE:

Song of Solomon chapter 2, verses 8-14

2   8 *"Listen! My beloved!*
Behold, he is coming,
Climbing on the mountains,
Leaping on the hills!"
9 *"My beloved is like a gazelle or a young stag.*
Behold, he is standing behind our wall,
He is looking though the windows,
He is peering through the lattice."   Not literal
10 *"My beloved responded and said to me,*
Arise, my darling, my beautiful one,
And come along."
11 *"For behold, the winter is past,*
The rain is over and gone."
12 *"The flowers have already appeared in the land;*
The time has arrived for pruning the vines,
And the voice of the turtledove has been heard in our land."
13 *"The fig tree has ripened its figs,*
And the vines in blossom have given forth their fragrance.
Arise, my darling, my beautiful one,
And come along!"

Life is florishing

Deepening *+* *Discovery*

14 *"O my dove, in the clefts of the rock,*
   In the secret place of the steep pathway,
   Let me see your form,
   Let me hear your voice;
   For your voice is sweet,
   And your form is lovely."

TEXT NOTES

Man creates trust in him + her.

TEXT QUESTIONS

1) What is the difference between courtship and dating?

2) To have a good courtship, what four things must occur?

3) What does, "Do you see honey? Eat what you need, lest you eat too much and vomit it up" and "Let your foot not often be in your neighbors house, lest he come to despise you" mean?

4) Song of Solomon 2:14, "O my dove, in the clefts of the rock..." What does this mean?

5) Ephesians 5:26, "...that He might sanctify her, having cleansed her by the washing of water with the word..." What does this verse mean?

 ## APPLICATION QUESTIONS

1) Tommy quotes, "you make your bed, then you have to lie in it," in reference to trying to change your partner after marriage. What is the principle Tommy is communicating?

2) According to Tommy, what needs to happen after having gone out for four to five weeks?

3) You can escalate your relationship too quickly by:
  *By sharing too much to fast
  *Putting your hands on your partner too fast
How can you avoid these two pitfalls?

4) Has your dating/marriage relationship made you further away from the Lord or has it produced life in your relationship with the Lord? How and why?

5) Unforgiveness is the root of pride and self righteousness. When was the last time you were unforgiving? Why?

When was the last time someone did not forgive you? How did that make you feel?

6) What do you need to do if your partner won't forgive your past before you are married?

7) How do you check yourself for the quality of forgiveness? How do you encourage your partner to do the same?

8) How do you cultivate the ability to see from another person's point of view?

9) In what way can you ensure that you are properly "evaluating" your partner to be suitable for you? How do you balance your love for another and your love for Christ?

10) Sometimes it is tempting to sweep difficulties under the rug. How are you developing the ability to speak openly and candidly with one another?

11) Why is it some get engaged in two weeks and some in five years? How do you deal with God's timetable for you?

12) Do you find yourself kissing another person before you are willing to hold his/her heart? Why?

13) Does your partner encourage you toward godliness or toward selfishness and greed?

KEY QUESTIONS

What was the most meaningful point you heard today? Why?

In light of what you have viewed today, how would you like to become more like this couple?

KEY THOUGHT

A great courtship leads to a great marriage. In order to have a godly marriage, strive for a godly courtship.

MEMORY VERSE

Proverbs 25:28
> "Like a city that is broken into and without walls is a man who has no control over his spirit."

PRAYER REQUESTS

SESSION FOUR
The Art of Courtship, Part II

INTRODUCTION

As the study of ***The Art of Courtship*** continues, Tommy brings our attention to the "little foxes" in a relationship. As a couple courts one another and draws closer to a point of ultimate commitment, the protection of the relationship is critical. This is a time when premarital sex most often can derail a good relationship. The two people are feeling very close to one another and truly believe they are in love. They must know that God's Word is very clear about sex before marriage. This is one of the most common "foxes" that can destroy a godly relationship.

SCRIPTURE:

Song of Solomon chapter 2, verses 15-17

2   15 *"Catch the foxes for us,*
The little foxes that are ruining the vineyards,
While our vineyards are in blossom."
16 *"My beloved is <u>mine</u>, and I am his;*
He pastures his flock among the lilies.
17 *"Until the cool of the day when the shadows flee away,*   *(ie) all night*
Turn, my beloved, and be like a gazelle   *Long*
Or a young stag on the mountains of Bether."

Psalm → 23

refers to her breasts

TEXT NOTES

We are more important Than me.
Sexual immorality makes you Think
you got more Than you got.

TEXT QUESTIONS

1) "Catch the foxes..." What does this mean?

2) What does Tommy mean when he quotes, "God can restore what the locust has eaten" and "He makes wine from water?"

3) Tommy mentions if he were an atheist he would tell you what three things?

4) In the text Tommy reads from Shakespeare, what is Prospero saying to Ferdinand?

5) Song of Solomon 2:16, "My beloved is mine, and I am his..." What does this mean?

 | **APPLICATION QUESTIONS**

1) There are two things you must do in your relationship to help it grow and keep the foxes out: TALK & LISTEN. Give a specific example of when you helped to keep the "foxes" out of your relationship.

2) How can you keep from being an incommunicable male/female?

How can you keep from being an apathetic partner?
i.e. "A is B and B is C, so therefore it won't work! Problem solved."
How can you encourage your partner from being this way?

3) Would your mate describe you as a sensitive or insensitive partner?
When was the last time you were vulnerable with your mate?

4) Do you stomp out and leave issues not reconciled? Why?

5) Song of Solomon 2:16b, "He pastures His flock among the lilies."
   What does this mean?

6) In this love story, who always takes the lead?

7) Men: Are you taking the lead in your relationship?
   Women: Are you allowing your partner to take the lead in your relationship?

8) Men: Give an example of how you last lead in your relationship.
   Women: Give an example of how you last allowed your partner to lead in your
      relationship.

9) If you have been faithful to God's plan, do you view this as a feather in your
   cap or God's grace? How does this affect your attitude in dealing with others?

10) Tommy would tell you these three things if he were an atheist. Give an
    example of how each one is harmful to you.
       *never borrow any money in excess:

       *never be unforgiving:

       *don't have premarital sex:

11) Can you give yourself completely to another? Compare this to your
    relationship with Christ.

KEY QUESTIONS

What was the most meaningful point you heard today? Why?

In light of what you have viewed today, how would you like to become more like this couple?

KEY THOUGHT

The three Golden Rules of Life by Tommy Nelson:
> Never borrow money in excess,
> Do not be an unforgiving person,
> Do not get involved in premarital sex.

MEMORY VERSE

Proverbs 5:18-19
> 18 "Let your fountain be blessed; And rejoice in the wife of your youth."
> 19 "As a loving hind and a graceful doe, Let her breasts satisfy you at all times; Be exhilarated always with her love."

PRAYER REQUESTS

SESSION FIVE
The Art of Intimacy, Part I

INTRODUCTION

The Art of Intimacy is the study of sex in a marriage. This lesson deals with those who waited for marriage to have sex and those who did not. Why is sex such a large part of life, yet people are afraid to talk and teach about it from God's Word? God created sex and He knows the best way for it to be enjoyed. The Art of Intimacy deals with who should take the lead in the relationship, how to have a godly wedding and how to be romantic.

SCRIPTURE:

Song of Solomon chapter 3, verses 1-11; chapter 4, verses 1-4

3 1 *"On my bed night after night I sought him*
Whom my soul loves;
I sought him but did not find him."
2 *"I must arise now and go about the city;*
In the streets and in the squares
I must seek him whom my soul loves.
I sought him but did not find him."
3 *"The watchmen who make the rounds in the city found me,*
And I said, 'Have you seen him whom my soul loves?'"
4 *"Scarcely had I left them*
When I found him whom my soul loves;
I held on to him and would not let him go,
Until I had brought him to my mother's house,
And into the room of her who conceived me."
5 *"I adjure you, O daughters of Jerusalem,*
By the gazelles or by the hinds of the field,
That you will not arouse or awaken love,
Until it pleases."

[handwritten annotations:] Her Soul loves him This is more Than just romance!

[handwritten annotation:] ← She doesn't want to wait anymore

6 "What is this coming up from the wilderness
Like columns of smoke,
Perfumed with myrrh and frankincense,
With all scented powders of the merchant?"
7 "Behold, it is the traveling couch of Solomon;
Sixty mighty men of Israel."
8 "All of them are wielders of the sword,
Expert in war;
Each man has his sword at his side,
Guarding against the terrors of the night."
9 "King Solomon has made for himself a sedan chariot
From the timber of Lebanon."
10 "He made its posts of silver,
Its back of gold
And its seat of purple fabric,
With its interior lovingly fitted out
By the daughter of Jerusalem."
11 "Go forth, O daughters of Zion,
And gaze on King Solomon with the crown
With which his mother has crowned him
On the day of his wedding,
And on the day of his gladness of heart."

4 1 "How beautiful you are, my darling,
How beautiful you are!
Your eyes are like doves behind your veil;
Your hair is like a flock of goats
That have descended from Mount Gilead."
2 "Your teeth are like a flock of newly shorn ewes
Which have come up from their washing,
All of which bear twins,
And not one among them has lost her young."
3 "Your lips are like a scarlet thread,
And your mouth is lovely.
Your temples are like a slice of pomegranate
Behind your veil."
4 "Your neck is like the tower of David
Built with rows of stones,
On which are hung a thousand shields,
All the round shields of mighty men."

TEXT NOTES

Man protects The woman
The country has born marriage to The ground.

TEXT QUESTIONS

1) Fill in these blanks:

_____ % of couples that live together get divorced.

_____ % of couples married by a justice of the peace get divorced.

_____ % of couples married in a church get divorced.

_____ out of _____ people who study their Bible get divorced.

2) Women are looking for men that have the strength of the cedars of Lebanon. What does that mean?

3) Song of Solomon 4:2, "Your teeth are like a flock of newly shorn ewes which have come up from their washing." What does this mean?

4) What does "Don't arouse and don't awaken love until it pleases" mean?

5) What is meant by "Passive men and wild women"?

 # APPLICATION QUESTIONS

1) How can you talk about sex in a godly manner?

2) Why do you think we don't talk about sex?

3) Do you believe God will bless your restraint for immediate gratification?

4) Where did you learn about sex?

5) Why is it that our society glorifies sex the way it does?

6) How have you or someone you know been hurt by sex?

7) How can you help to keep yourself and your partner pure?

   If you have had sex, how can you start again today?

8) Why do we try to sweep the issue of sex under the rug?

9) In your list of priorities, how important is your "word"?

10) How do you assure objectiveness in evaluating the person you're dating? Your spouse?

11) Do you feel secure in your relationship with Christ?
    If no, how can you be secure in your marriage?

    If yes, how does it affect your relationship?

12) Are you keeping your standards high or lowering them in order to get married, for fear that life is passing you by?

13) In what other areas of your life are you keeping your standards high?

In what areas are you "selling out?"

14) Give an example of how you've seen the cliché "men use romance to get sex and women use sex to get romance."

15) Give an example of when you last shared at a "level three" (a deep level)?

16) What was the last thing you did that was romantic?

17) If someone were to be romantic toward you, what would you want them to do?

KEY QUESTIONS

What was the most meaningful point you heard today? Why?

In light of what you have viewed today, how would you like to become more like this couple?

KEY THOUGHT

"The first key to great sex is called romance."

MEMORY VERSE

Proverbs 5:18-19

18 "Let your fountain be blessed; And rejoice in the wife of your youth."
19 "As a loving hind and a graceful doe, Let her breasts satisfy you at all times; Be exhilarated always with her love."

PRAYER REQUESTS

Shepard King

SESSION SIX
The Art of Intimacy, Part II

INTRODUCTION

The Art of Intimacy addresses sex between a married couple. Tommy will answer such questions as: Should a couple talk about sex before they get married? What to do on the honeymoon night? How do I be with my spouse? What signals are there? and What does a man and a woman look for in sex? This is the straight talking and biblical discussion that people want and need to hear. Tommy's candor and experience bring light to his discussion of Solomon and the Shulamite woman.

SCRIPTURE:

Song of Solomon chapter 4, verses 5-16

4   5 *"Your two breasts are like two fawns,*
Twins of a gazelle,
Which feed among the lilies."
6 *"Until the cool of the day*
When the shadows flee away,
I will go my way the mountain of myrrh   *}building steam*
And to the hill of frankincense."

Ephesians →   7 *"You are altogether beautiful, my darling,*
And there is no blemish in you."
8 *"Come with me from Lebanon, my bride,*
May you come with me from Lebanon.
Journey down from the summit Amana,
From the summit of Senir and Hermon,   *Scary place where*
From the dens of lions,   *lion would build*
From the mountains of leopards.   *their dens*
9 *"You have made my heart beat faster, my sister, my bride;*
You have made my heart beat faster with a single glance of your eyes,
With a single strand of your necklace."
10 *"How beautiful is your love, my sister, my bride!*
How much better is your love than wine,

And the fragrance of your oils
Than all kinds of spices!"
11 *"Your lips, my bride, drip honey;* ← First Kiss
Honey and milk are under your tongue,
And the fragrance of your garments is like the fragrance of Lebanon."
12 *"A garden locked is my sister, my bride,*
A rock garden locked, a spring sealed up." → Never been before
13 *"Your shoots are an orchard of pomegranates*
With choice fruits, henna with nard plants,
14 *Nard and saffron, calamus and cinnamon,*
With all the trees of frankincense,
Myrrh and aloes, along with all the finest spices."
15 *"You are a garden spring,*
A well of fresh water,
And streams flowing from Lebanon."
16 *"Awake, O north wind,* ← Prayer request"
And come, wind of the south;
Make my garden breathe out fragrance,
Let its spices be wafted abroad.
May my beloved come into his garden
And eat its choice fruits!"
5:1 *"I have come into my garden, my sister, my bride;*
I have gathered my myrrh along with my balsam.
I have eaten my honeycomb and my honey;
I have drunk my wine and my milk."

TEXT NOTES

Law of deminishing returns

Throughout book sensuality is referred to as
  a garden.

Great Sex
1) Know the difference between a male and a female
2) A man enjoys responsiveness, Know what is good sex
   A woman enjoys / tenderness
3) Start early - romance is an all day event; prepare her heart
4) learn your mates signals
5) Beware of Combinations
6) Learn Boundaries

34

TEXT QUESTIONS

1) What is the verse for the woman to memorize, but for the man to never quote?

2) "The _____ _____ can change your life and the _____ can illumine your way."

3) What are the ten points Tommy gives on sex in marriage?

    1)

    2)

    3)

    4)

    5)

    6)

    7)

    8)

    9)

    10)

4) Song of Solomon 5:1,
    "I have come into my garden, my sister, my bride;
    I have gathered my myrrh along with my balsam.
    I have eaten my honeycomb and my honey;
    I have drunk my wine and my milk."

What is the word that is mentioned nine times?

5) On your honeymoon, you move _____.

 APPLICATION QUESTIONS

1) In dating: Which question do you ask yourself:
"How far can I go in sex?" or "How far can I stay away from sex?"

2) What situations are especially dangerous with a dating partner? What can you do to help keep each other accountable?

3) What does Tommy make couples do before they marry?

4) How can we be open in our communication about sex when most have been "trained" not to talk about it?

5) Do you have signals with your partner? What are they?

6) How can signals be healthy in a relationship?

7) There are three things Tommy mentions that bring excitement to a man:
　　　*What he hears
　　　*What he sees
　　　*What he feels

　　Why is it important for a woman to know these?

8) What consummates a marriage?

9) "A woman does not have authority over her own body, but the man does." I Corinthians 7:4 is the verse for the woman to memorize, but for the man to never quote. Why?

10) Do you and your husband/wife pray after having sex? Will you commit to doing this?

11) "The Holy Spirit can change your life and the Bible can illumine your way." How are you allowing this to happen in your life? Specifically, how can you make this more apparent in your life?

12) We are to fear the consequences of sex outside of God's will. How do we help to minimize the fear of sex that God ordains in marriage?

13) Song of Solomon 5:1,
　　　"I have come into my garden, my sister, my bride;
　　　I have gathered my myrrh along with my balsam.
　　　I have eaten my honeycomb and my honey;
　　　I have drunk my wine and my milk."
What does Tommy say about the recurring word "my" in this text?

14) How does the possessive nature of marriage make you feel?

KEY QUESTIONS

What was the most meaningful point you heard today? Why?

In light of what you have viewed today, how would you like to become more like this couple?

KEY THOUGHT

"Great sex takes great communication. In order for a married couple's sex life to be fulfilling for a lifetime, they must talk."

MEMORY VERSE

Ephesians 4:29

"Let no unwholesome word proceed from your mouth, but only such a word is good for edification according to the need of the moment, that it may give grace to those who hear."

PRAYER REQUESTS

SESSION SEVEN
The Art of Conflict, Part I

INTRODUCTION

The Art of Conflict deals with perhaps the most important aspect of any relationship—fighting. As Tommy says, "All couples fight; good couples fight clean and bad couples fight dirty." What does it mean to fight clean or dirty? This question and many others will be answered in this lesson. Notice that this section comes right on the heels of The Art of Intimacy. About 25 percent of the book deals with sex, and about 25 percent of the book deals with conflict. Just as a thunderstorm can be very destructive to land, so can conflict be to your relationship. Like a storm ending with a rainbow, so may your conflict end.

SCRIPTURE:

Song of Solomon chapter 5, verses 1-9; chapter 6, verses 1-13

5 1 *"I have come into my garden, my sister, my bride;*
I have gathered my myrrh along with balsam.
I have eaten my honeycomb and my honey;
I have drunk my wine and my milk.
Eat, friends;
Drink and imbibe deeply, O lovers."
2 *"I was asleep, but my heart was awake.*
A voice! My beloved was knocking:
Open to me, my sister, my darling,
My dove, my perfect one!
For my head is drenched with dew,
My locks with the damp of the night."
3 *"I have taken off my dress,*
How can I put it on again?
I have washed my feet,
How can I dirty them again?"
4 *"My beloved extended his hand through the opening,*
And my feelings were aroused for him."

handwritten note: Someone else Speaks God!!

handwritten note: Go away

handwritten note: Responds in Gentleness

5 "I arose to open to my beloved;
And my hands dripped with myrrh,
And my fingers with liquid myrrh,
On the handles of the bolt."
6 "I opened to my beloved,
But my beloved had turned away and had gone!
My heart went out to him as he spoke. — He recalls his words
I searched for him, but I did not find him;
I called him, but he did not answer me."
7 "The watchmen who make the rounds in the city found me,
They struck me and wounded me; } God humbles me
The guardsmen of the walls took away my shawl from me."
8 "I adjure you, O daughters of Jerusalem,
If you find my beloved,
As to what you will tell him:
For I am lovesick."
9 "What kind of beloved is your beloved,
O most beautiful among women?
What kind of beloved is your beloved,
That thus you adjure us?"

6 1 "Where has your beloved gone,
O most beautiful among women?
Where has your beloved turned,
That we may seek him with you?"
2 "My beloved has gone down to his garden,
To the beds of balsam,
To pasture his flock in the gardens
And gather lilies." — she knows where he is!
3 "I am my beloved's and my beloved is mine,
He who pastures his flock among the lilies."
4 "You are as beautiful as
Tizrah, my darling,
As lovely as Jerusalem,
As awesome as an army
with banners."
5 "Turn your eyes away from me, → Best line
For they have confused me;
Your hair is like a flock of goats
That have descended from Gilead."
6 "Your teeth are like a flock of ewes
Which have come up form their washing,
All of which bear twins,
And not one among them has lost her young."
7 "Your temples are like a slice of pomegranate
Behind your veil."

40

8 "There are sixty queens and eighty concubines,
And maidens without number;
9 "But my dove, my perfect one, is unique:
She is her mother's only daughter;
She is the pure child of the one who bore her.
The maidens saw her and called her blessed,
The queens and the concubines also, and they praised her, saying,
10 'Who is this that grows like the dawn,
As beautiful as the full moon,
As pure as the sun,
As awesome as an army with banners?'
11 "I went down to the orchard of nut trees
To see the blossoms of the valley,
To see whether the vine had budded
Or the pomegranates had bloomed." — Solomon
12 "Before I was aware, my soul set me
Over the chariots of my noble people." — female equivalent to Solomon
13 "Come back, come back, O Shulamite;
Come back, come back, that we may gaze at you."
"Why should you gaze at the Shulamite,
As at the dance of the two companies?"

TEXT NOTES

1) Do not react to your mate 5:4
2) Do try to change your mate, let God change your mate in The light of your grace
3) You have resolution
4) Forgiveness
6) Reconciliation

Conflict is like dust, it has to settle Someplace
Maturity - yielding to the Standard of God

James Dobson
Proverbs : a harsh word starts up anger

TEXT QUESTIONS

1) Conflict is _____% of the book. This is prophetic, because marriage is
   about _____% of conflict.

2) According to Tommy, what is exposed when "bad couples" conflict?
   What is exposed when "good couples" conflict?

Point to conflict
1) do not raise your voice
2) never publically embarrass

3) What does the word "meanness" mean?

3) Not infront of kids
4) Never use your kids
5) Never use always or Never
6) Never call names
7) Don't get historical

4) What is meant by calling the woman the "weaker vessel?"

8) Don't leave Angry
9) Never freeze out your mate
10) Don't use Sex
11) Don't use the inlaws
12) Never use reason

5) It is the _____ _____ job to change my partner, not mine.

13) Don't interrupt your mate
14) Don't fail to listen
15) Never touch in Anger
16) Never reverse arguments

APPLICATION QUESTIONS

1) Give an example of a time when you were in conflict and your:
   *Character was exposed: *17) Never harden yourself*

42

* Your immaturity was exposed:

2) Those who don't conflict in marriage either don't communicate or there is one person dominating and one subdued. Are you either of these? What do you need to do to improve here?

3) Why are marriages without conflict unhealthy?

4) In conflict, do you repay evil with evil?

5) In conflict, do you react to your mate? Give an example of a time you reacted hot (in anger) or cold (shutting your partner out, leaving him/her to walk on egg shells).

6) How do you know when you have hurt your mate?

7) What does Tommy mean when he says "You can't use the forgiveness of your mate as an excuse to hurt him/her, because you are going to wound your partner, as well as yourself."

8) It is the Holy Spirit's job to change my partner, not mine. My job is to:

9) How can your trust in God be great enough to allow Him to make changes where changes are needed?

10) How does this conversation between Pilate and Jesus apply to your relationship: "'Don't you know I have the power to release you and I have the power to crucify you?' He said to him, 'You have no authority unless my Father in heaven gives it to you.'"?

11) Do you find it easy to put other's needs off because of selfishness? Or are you ignoring your own needs? How can you find a healthy balance?

12) How have you shown humility to make the first move toward reconciliation with your partner? Are you always the last to reconcile?

13) Are you aware of your non-verbal communication? Are you aware of others' non-verbal communication? Give some examples.

KEY QUESTIONS

What was the most meaningful point you heard today? Why?

In light of what you have viewed today, how would you like to become more like this couple?

KEY THOUGHT

"Every couple fights! Do you press for a victory or for a resolution?"

MEMORY VERSE

I Peter 3:9

> "...not returning evil for evil, or insult for insult, but giving a blessing instead; for you were called for the very purpose that you might inherit a blessing."

PRAYER REQUESTS

SESSION EIGHT
The Art of Conflict, Part II

INTRODUCTION

The Art of Conflict deals with turning conflict into intimacy and joy. Some key issues in dealing with problems in any relationship is how to listen and how to handle different types of people. When people get married, they bring different thoughts, views, opinions and other aspects together. We are like two blocks of granite, each barely seeing and knowing more than just the faint highlight of the other. Marriage, with all of its joys and struggles, allows the two blocks to have friction on each other. As this continues to happen, each person is revealed more and more. Marriage without conflict would be superficial and stale, but with friction, the most beautiful statue of two people may be created.

SCRIPTURE:

Song of Solomon chapter 5, verses 10-16; chapter 6, verses 1-13

5 10 *"My beloved is dazzling and ruddy,*
Outstanding among ten thousand."
11 "His head is like gold, pure gold;
His locks are like clusters of dates,
And black as a raven."
12 "His eyes are like doves,
Beside streams of water,
Bathed in milk,
And reposed in their setting."
13 "His cheeks are like a bed of balsam,
Banks of sweet-scented herbs;
His lips are lilies,
Dripping with liquid myrrh."
14 "His hands are rods of gold
Set with beryl;
His abdomen is carved ivory
Inlaid with sapphires."

15 *"His legs are pillars of alabaster*
Set on pedestals of pure gold;
His appearance is like Lebanon,
Choice as the cedars."
16 *"His mouth is full of sweetness.*
And he is wholly desirable.
This is my beloved and this is my friend,
O daughters of Jerusalem."

6

1 *"Where has your beloved gone,*
O most beautiful among women?
Where has your beloved turned,
That we may seek him with you?"
2 *"My beloved has gone down to his garden,*
To the beds of balsam,
To pasture his flock in the gardens
And gather lilies."
3 *"I am my beloved's and my beloved is mine,*
He who pastures his flock among the lilies."
4 *"You are as beautiful as*
Tizrah, my darling,
As lovely as Jerusalem,
As awesome as an army
with banners."
5 *"Turn your eyes away from me,*
For they have confused me;
Your hair is like a flock of goats
That have descended from Gilead."
6 *"Your teeth are like a flock of ewes*
Which have come up from their washing,
All of which bear twins,
And not one among them has lost her young."
7 *"Your temples are like a slice of pomegranate*
Behind your veil."
8 *"There are sixty queens and eighty concubines,*
And maidens without number;
9 *"But my dove, my perfect one, is unique:*
She is her mother's only daughter;
She is the pure child of the one who bore her.
The maidens saw her and called her blessed,
The queens and the concubines also, and they praised her, saying,
10 *'Who is this that grows like the dawn,*
As beautiful as the full moon,
As pure as the sun,
As awesome as an army with banners?'

11 *"I went down to the orchard of nut trees*

To see the blossoms of the valley,
To see whether the vine had budded
Or the pomegranates had bloomed."
12 "Before I was aware, my soul set me
Over the chariots of my noble people."
13 "Come back, come back, O Shulamite;
Come back, come back, that we may gaze at you."
"Why should you gaze at the Shulamite,
As at the dance of the two companies?"

 ## TEXT NOTES

 ## TEXT QUESTIONS

1) What does Tommy teach about the word "reposed?"

2) Micah 7:18, "Because He delights in unchanging love." What does this mean?

3) What are the four major problems in a marriage?

     1)

     2)

     3)

     4)

4) Conflict brings _____ and _____ .

5) Song of Solomon 6:12, "...my soul set me over the chariots of my noble people." What does this mean?

A | APPLICATION QUESTIONS

1) When your partner has "done you wrong," there are three things Tommy tells you not to do:
     *Don't run home to your mother
     *Don't stomp out the door
     *Don't go off with your friends and talk about him/her
Give an example of when you did one of these three things.

What is a better way to handle conflict?

2) Song of Solomon 5:10, "My beloved is dazzling and ruddy, Outstanding among ten thousand." What does this mean?

3) "Reposed" means the man's eyes don't ever change. They never narrow in anger. How can you be more like this man?

4) According to Tommy, the four major problems in a marriage are:

   *The man's mother
   *The woman's mother
   *sex
   *money

Give an example of each and how you could see it causing problems in your relationship.

5) Who deals with the woman's parents when they are causing conflict? Who deals with the man's parents when they are causing conflict? Why?

6) Clara Barton, head of the Red Cross, was asked about somebody that had hurt her. She replied, "I distinctly remember forgetting that." When you forgive another, do you forget?

7) Conflict brings intimacy and joy. Give an example of a time this has happened in your relationships.

8) How can you have the same receptacle of grace towards others that Jesus Christ has for you?

9) Tommy mentions twelve things not to do when communicating with your mate:

1 - don't speak rashly
2 - don't confront your mate publicly
3 - don't confront your mate before the kids
4 - don't use the kids
5 - don't say "you never..." or "you always..."
6 - don't get historical
7 - don't raise your voice
8 - don't call names
9 - don't mention family
10 - don't win
11 - don't condescend
12 - don't demean

10) What problems do have in your relationships? Be specific.

11) Tommy mentions seven ways to listen to your mate:

1 - listen with your face
2 - do not reason with your mate
3 - do not argue
4 - do not interrupt
5 - do not stomp out the door
6 - do not vent your spleen to others
7 - use no rude body language

What would your mate say about your listening skills?

12) In God's sovereign plan, He can use sin in our lives to mold us and to give us wisdom. Even though sin is harmful we are forgiven and can become wiser. Do you feel forgiven and wiser or do you feel condemned? Why?

KEY QUESTIONS

What was the most meaningful point you heard today? Why?

In light of what you have viewed today, how would you like to become more like this couple?

 KEY THOUGHT

"Before you get straight with your mate, get straight with your Maker."

 MEMORY VERSE

Ecclesiastes 9:9

"Enjoy life with the woman whom you love all the days of your fleeting life which he has given to you under the sun; for this is your reward in life, and in your toil in which you have labored under the sun."

 PRAYER REQUESTS

SESSION NINE
The Art of Romance, Part I

INTRODUCTION

If Tommy had only one lesson to teach people about love, sex, marriage and romance, it would be ***The Art of Romance.*** So many marriages fail because two people become forgetful and lazy. A picture of The Art of Romance is that of a gardener. When someone decides to plant a garden, there is the thrill of seeing how beautiful it will become. The appreciation and enjoyment of it lasts for a season. But inevitably, weeds and other destructive forces begin to take their toll on the flowers and foods. Does the gardener sit back, watch this happen and wish for it to die? Like a gardener, you and your partner must work to improve and protect your relationship. In this portion of The Art of Romance, let's see how Tommy teaches us to do this.

SCRIPTURE:

Song of Solomon chapter 7, verse 1-2 & 11

7 1 *"How beautiful are your feet in sandals,*
O prince's daughter!
The curves of your hips are like jewels,
The work of the hands of an artist."
2 *"Your navel is like a round goblet*
Which never lacks mixed wine;
Your belly is like a heap of wheat
Fenced about with lilies."
Vs. 11, *"Come, my beloved, let us go out into the country,*
Let us spend the night in the villages."

TEXT NOTES

TEXT QUESTIONS

1) Proverbs 31:31, "Give her the product of her hands." What does this mean?

2) _____ % of high school students can't imagine their parents having sex. Why?

3) "Marriages do not devolve. That is a worldly idea, it's not biblical."
   What does this mean?

4) Tommy says "You may not think you are Romeo, but you are marrying Juliet." What does this mean?

5) Song of Solomon 7:2, "Your belly is like a heap of wheat." What dos this mean?

 APPLICATION QUESTIONS

1) There are four horsemen to marriage that you will deal with:

    1) Sin   What does this mean?

    2) Age   What does this mean?

    3) Forgetfulness   What does this mean?

    4) Laziness   What does this mean?

2) The first four of ten things that deepen a relationship are:

    1) Your knowledge of your mate. Give an example of this:

    2) Your exaltation deepens. Give an example of this:

    3) Your praise goes up. Give an example of this:

4) Your appreciation goes up. Give an example of this:

3) How are you giving your partner the product of his/her hands?

4) Josh McDowell says "The problem with immorality is that you think you got more than you got." What does this mean?

5) "The man is the leader of romance." What are you doing to lead in this area? How can you encourage your partner to be romantic too?

6) Why are a lot of men only romantic on special occasions? What does it mean "to feel prostituted"?

How can you prevent this from happening in your relationship? Be specific.

7) How do you take the time to study your significant other? What are his/her dreams, desires, fears, doubts?

8) How do you admire your partner more today than yesterday?

Does your partner admire you more?

What can you do to deepen your admiration toward one another?

9) If you are married, do you and your partner have a date night? Make a list of some things you and your mate can do on a date night. (Be romantic.)

10) Do you believe you can leave your parents and cleave to your mate? What is a healthy way to do this?

FOCUS POINT

Though shall not commit adultery. Exodus 20:14

ADULTERY...

"...strengthen the hands of evildoers..." Jeremiah 23:14
"...not inherit the kingdom of God..." I Corinthians 6:9
"He who would destroy himself does it." Proverbs 6:23b

The writer of Proverbs teaches in chapter 6, verse 23:

"For the commandment is a lamp, and the teaching is light;
And reproofs for discipline are the way of life..."

Tommy gives us the six "E's" to having an affair. These are not a formula but a strong warning. May you pray and commit to see God's commandment as a lamp and this teaching as a light in your life.

11) What would God say about how you handle your money?

12) Do you practice passive behavior when your partner doesn't agree with you (e.g. rolling your eyes, sighing, ignoring the person, etc.)?

Does your partner do this with you? How does this behavior make you feel?

What can you do to keep each other accountable in this area?

13) The six "E's" of how to have an affair are:

1) Elimination   example:

2) Encounter   example:

3) Enjoyment   example:

4) Expedition   example:

5) Expression   example:

6) Experience   example:

Why do they all begin with the letter E?

14) How can you help to protect your marriage from an affair?

KEY QUESTIONS

What was the most meaningful point you heard today? Why?

In light of what you have viewed today, how would you like to become more like this couple?

KEY THOUGHT

"You are made to be romantic. God is romantic."

MEMORY VERSE

Ecclesiastes 9:9
"Enjoy life with the woman whom you love all the days of your fleeting life which he has given to you under the sun; for this is your reward in life, and in your toil in which you have labored under the sun."

PRAYER REQUESTS

SESSION TEN
The Art of Romance, Part II

INTRODUCTION

What is romance? Is it only bringing flowers or doing little things? Is it always being spontaneous and showing your love for your mate in new and different ways? Although these things are very important in building and keeping romance alive in a marriage, there are many other aspects that add to the deepening of an intimate relationship. In this session, **The Art of Romance, Part II,** you will see that this couple knows the joy of romance. This couple does not get bored with one another. His appreciation of her is a constant process, just as her respect for him grows greater everyday.

SCRIPTURE:

Song of Solomon chapter 7, verses 3-13; chapter 8, verses 1-3

7 3 *"Your two breasts are like two fawns,*
Twins of a gazelle."
4 *"Your neck is like a tower of ivory,*
Your eyes like the pools in Heshbon } you are refreshing
By the gate of Bathrabbim;
Your nose is like the tower of Lebanon, ← you don't shame me
Which faces toward Damascus."
5 *"Your head crowns you like Carmel,* ← Her beauty
And the flowing locks of your head are like purple threads;
The king is captivated by your tresses."
6 *"How beautiful and how delightful you are,*
My love, with all your charms!" (i.e) Softness
7 *"Your stature is like a palm tree,*
And your breasts are like its clusters."
8 *"I said, 'I will climb the palm tree,*
I will take hold of its fruit stalks.'
Oh, may your breasts be like clusters of the vine,

And the fragrance of your breath like apples,
9 "And your mouth like the best wine!"
It goes down smoothly for my beloved,
Flowing gently through the lips of those who fall asleep."
10 "I am my beloved's,
And his desire is for me."
11 "Come, my beloved, let us go out into the country,
Let us spend the night in the villages."
12 "Let us rise early and go to the vineyards;
Let us see whether the vine has budded
And its blossoms have opened,
And whether the pomegranates have bloomed.
There I will give you my love."
13 "The mandrakes have given forth fragrance;
And over our doors are all choice fruits,
Both new and old,
Which I have saved up for you, my beloved."

8 1 "Oh that you were like a brother to me
Who nursed at my mother's breasts.
If I found you outdoors, I would kiss you;
No one would despise me, either."
2 "I would lead you and bring you
Into the house of my mother who used to instruct me;
I would give you spiced wine to drink from the juice of my pomegranates."
3 "Let his left hand be under my head,
And his right hand embrace me."

Handwritten margin notes:
- The woman's juice
- She aggresive
- Viagra Expressions
- She is created
- modesty
- my mom Taught me about sex
- She is Spontaneous

T TEXT NOTES

Handwritten:

1) be courteous,
2) be together
3) Be expressive - to your mate
4) Be affectionate
5) Be creative
6) Be Thoughtful
7) Be Insightful to the needs of your mate
8) Be energetic

TEXT QUESTIONS

1) What does NST stand for?

2) What does "Your neck is like an ivory tower." mean?

3) Historically, what does "Your eyes are like the pools in Heshbon by the gate of Bath-rabbim" mean?

4) Historically, what does "Your nose is like the tower of Lebanon, which faces toward Damascus" mean?

5) Historically, what does "Your head crowns you like Carmel" mean?

APPLICATION QUESTIONS

1) How does "Your eyes are like the pools in Heshbon by the gate of Bath-rabbim;"apply to you?

Does this describe you and your partner? Does this describe your relationship with Christ? How can you have more of this in your life?

2) How does "Your nose is like the tower of Lebanon, Which faces toward Damascus." apply to you?

Does this describe you and your partner? Does this describe your relationship with Christ?

How can you have more of this in your life?

3) How does "Your head crowns you like Carmel" apply to you?

Does this describe you and your partner? Does this describe your relationship with Christ?

How can you have more of this in your life?

4) "Your head crowns you like Carmel, and the flowing locks of your head are like purple threads." How did they get purple dye in that day?

Purple was the color of what?

5) The previous verse shows Solomon's admiration for his wife. How can you show your mate the same kind of admiration?

6) If you are married, do you treat your mate with the same tenderness and appreciation sexually as you did on your honeymoon? Why or Why not?

7) According to Tommy, what does it mean for a woman to be "fussy"? How can you keep from becoming this kind of woman?

8) What can you do to be more responsive to your mate's needs?

9) What does it mean to become stagnant in a relationship?

Are you stagnant? Does your mate see you as stagnant?

10) What can you do to overcome staleness in your relationship?

11) How much fun are you to be with?

In what areas of your life can you become a more pleasant and fun person?

12) The last six things that deepen a relationship are:

1) Your respect deepens.　　　　Give an example:

2) Your delight deepens.　　　　Give an example:

3) Your trust deepens.　　　　Give an example:

4) Your admiration deepens.　　Give an example:

5) Your devotion deepens.　　　Give an example:

6) Your passion deepens.　　　Give an example:

13) Romantic times are not going to happen every day, as some of us would like. So how can you pray every day that God make you a more romantic partner?

KEY QUESTIONS

What was the most meaningful point you heard today? Why?

In light of what you have viewed today, how would you like to become more like this couple?

KEY THOUGHT

Love is a discipline. Love is a choice.

MEMORY VERSE

Ecclesiastes 9:9
> "Enjoy life with the woman whom you love all the days of your fleeting life which he has given to you under the sun; for this is your reward in life, and in your toil in which you have labored under the sun."

PRAYER REQUESTS

SESSION ELEVEN
The Art of Commitment, Part I

INTRODUCTION

The Art of Commitment is having the perseverance and perspective to make your marriage last a lifetime. For example, when a person is learning to sky dive he must be committed to jump out of the plane long before ever getting into it. If a person is not committed to jump, think of the very tempting option to scream, "Forget it!" The fear of the jump would paralyze him and he would never experience the joy and rush of "flying." Marriage and commitment is much the same. Divorce is not an option, and it must not be one from the day a person says "I do." If divorce is an option, many people will take it. So as Christ intended, stay committed for a lifetime and He will give you and your partner abundant joy.

SCRIPTURE:

Song of Solomon chapter 8, verses 4-9

8 4 *"I want you to swear, O daughters of Jerusalem,*
Do not arouse or awaken my love,
Until she pleases."
5 *"Who is this coming up from the wilderness,*
Leaning on her beloved?"
"Beneath the apple tree I awakened you;
There your mother was in labor with you,
There she was in labor and gave you birth."
6 *"Put me like a <u>seal</u> over <u>your heart</u>,*
Like a <u>seal</u> on <u>your arm</u>.
For love is as strong as death,
Jealousy is as severe as Sheol;
Its flashes are flashes of fire,
The very flame of the Lord."
7 *"Many waters cannot quench love,*
Nor will rivers overflow it;
If a man were to give all the riches of his house for love,

[handwritten: Providential you were born for me.]

[handwritten: I am not sharing you →]

It would be utterly despised."
8 "We have a little sister,
And she has no breasts;
What shall we do for our sister   ← Father is gone
On the day when she is spoken for?"
9 "If she is a wall,   ← mature enough to be moral
We shall build on her battlement of silver;
But if she is a door,
We shall barricade her with planks of cedar."

TEXT NOTES

TEXT QUESTIONS

1) "To have and to hold from this day forward, for better or for worse, for richer or for poorer, in sickness and in health, to love, honor and cherish, forsaking all others to keep you only unto myself so long as we both shall live. In the name of the Father and of the Son and of the Holy Spirit." What does this mean?

2) "Thou shalt not take the name of the Lord Thy God in vain." The two areas Tommy mentions are:

3) "God made them male and God made them female and what God joins together, no human may separate." What does this mean?

4) "If she is a wall, we shall build on her a battlement of silver." What does this mean?

5) From 1900 to 1980, the divorce rate rose _____ %.

A | APPLICATION QUESTIONS

1) "Thou shalt not take the name of the Lord thy God in vain." The two areas Tommy mentions are:
    *cursing
    *not keeping your word

What is an oath?

Give an example of when you broke an oath. How did this make you and the other person feel?

2) Is your loving treatment of your mate of a higher ratio than that of your saying "I'm sorry"?

How can you improve this ratio in your relationship? Be specific.

3) "There your mother was in labor with you, there she was in labor and gave you birth." According to Tommy, how does this verse apply to you and your mate?

4) "Put me like a seal over your heart, like a seal on your arm." What does she mean?

What does a seal portray?

5) "For love is as strong as death, Jealousy is as severe as Sheol." What does this mean?

Why is love permanent?

6) "Its flashes are flashes of fire, The very flame of the Jehovah." What does this mean?

7) "Many waters cannot quench love, Nor will rivers overflow it." What does this mean?

In your relationship, is there anything that could quench your love?

8) What is the story of Hosea and the love he had for his wife? How can your love be more like this?

9) "If a man were to give all the riches of his house for love, it would be utterly despised" means do not marry/date another just for their money. What are the pitfalls of marrying/dating someone for their money?

If Christ only loved you for your money/material things, how would this impact you?

10) "If she is a wall, we shall build on her a battlement of silver" means she is closed off to men sexually. She is not immoral. She will not sell out her virginity. How can you be this kind of woman?

11) "A girl is ready to be married when she is willing to stay single before she will disobey God." Discuss this statement and how it could change your life.

KEY QUESTIONS

What was the most meaningful point you heard today? Why?

In light of what you have viewed today, how would you like to become more like this couple?

KEY THOUGHT

Let your "yes" mean yes and your "no" mean no.

MEMORY VERSE

Matthew 19:6
"Consequently they are no longer two, but one flesh. What therefore God has joined together, let no man separate."

PRAYER REQUESTS

SESSION TWELVE
The Art of Commitment, Part II

INTRODUCTION

The Art of Commitment Part II, will finish this incredible love story. Perhaps the most important aspect of this section is the sovereignty of God in our lives. God is the all-knowing, the all-loving, and the all-powerful One. He is the creator of all and He knows what is best for everyone. It is God who brings this couple from initial attraction to the joy of sex to a lifelong commitment. In order to have a godly marriage, Jesus Christ must be your Lord and Savior. This session is about being committed to God and then to one another. You can enjoy God's best in His institution of marriage.

SCRIPTURE:
Song of Solomon chapter 8, verses 10-14

8 10 "I was a wall, and my breasts were like towers;
Then I became in his eyes as one who finds peace."
11 "Solomon had a vineyard at Baal-hamon;
He entrusted the vineyard to caretakers;
Each one was to bring a thousand shekels of silver for its fruit."
12 "My very own vineyard is at my disposal;
The thousand shekels are for you, Solomon,
And two hundred are for those who take care of its fruit."
13 "O you who sit in the gardens,
My companions are listening for your voice,
Let me hear it!"
14 "Hurry, my beloved,
And be like a gazelle or a young stag
On the mountains of spices."

For her brother who took care of you →

Malachi chapter 2, verses 13-16

2 13 "And this is another thing you do: you cover the
altar of the Lord with tears,
with weeping and with groaning, because He no longer regards
the offering or accepts it with favor from your hand."
14 "Yet you say, 'For what reason?' Because the Lord has
been a witness between you and the wife of your youth, against whom
you have dealt treacherously, though she is your companion and your
wife by covenant."
15 "But not one has done so who has a remnant of the Spirit. And what
did that one do while he was seeking a godly offering? Take heed then, to
your spirit, and let no one deal treacherously against the wife of your youth."
16 "For I hate divorce," says the Lord, the God of Israel, "and him who
covers his garment with wrong," says the Lord of hosts. "So take heed to
your spirit, that you do not deal treacherously."

TEXT NOTES

Safest place to be - in The
will of God

TEXT QUESTIONS

1) "...then I became in his eyes as one who finds peace.." What does this mean?

2) Why did Tommy want the fathers to circle the verse, "And two hundred (meaning shekels) are for those who take care of its fruit"?

3) How does Tommy apply Malachi 2:13-16 to your relationship with your mate?

4) The Bible says "By grace you have been saved through faith..." What does this mean?

5) What are the five truths Tommy mentions?

      1)

      2)

      3)

      4)

      5)

APPLICATION QUESTIONS

1) "My mother's sons were angry with me; They made me caretaker of the vineyards..." Did she want to work in the vineyard?

How can you relate to her?

2) Do you think your parents are too hard on you? Why?

3) Are you glad your parents are hard on you? Why?

4) How would you be as a parent?

5) Tommy says, "Get in the path that a woman is in for that kind of man to be looking for. Are you in the path you that you would want your mate to be in?

6) God providentially took care of her body. God providentially takes care of your body. How can you see this in your life?

7) "When you are taking out a Christian girl/guy you are taking out God's daughter/son." Why is this convicting?

8) How can you go into your marriage without a weak link (knowing that when it gets tough neither of you will run)?

9) "...then I became in his eyes as one who finds peace..." How do you have "peace" with your mate?

10) What does Tommy mention is the last act of love?

11) "Heaven is free." What does this mean?

12) "The blood of Jesus Christ who died in your place can wash you clean of everything you've ever done." Do you believe this? Why?

13) If God asked you, "Why should I let you stand in my presence?" what would you say?

14) If you were to die right now, do you know for certain you would be with God in heaven? Why?

15) When all religions are broken down, there are only two kinds. What does each mean?

   *Manianity:

   *Christianity:

KEY QUESTIONS

What was the most meaningful point you heard today? Why?

In light of what you have viewed today, how would you like to become more like this couple?

 ## KEY THOUGHT

The reason you keep the finite, is because you know the infinite.

 ## MEMORY VERSE

Matthew 19:6

"Consequently they are no longer two, but one flesh. What therefore God has joined together, let no man separate.

 ## PRAYER REQUESTS

Appendix

Answers to Song of Solomon Text Questions

Text Answers Session 1:
1. 1) Genesis through Nehemiah
2) Esther through Song of Solomon
3) Isaiah through Malachi
2) *servant to God
*believer in God
3) A man's name is a man's character
4) She obeyed the authority over her
5) This is what the whores did. Wearing veils, they would follow after the flock and give themselves to the shepherds.

Text Answers Session 2:

1) *flesh
*lusts
2) Inner beauty is where a person finds respect.
3) He is proud of her and he protects her.
4) This refers to the sexual position
5) Physical love is not to be aroused in any form, until a couple is married.

Text Answers Session 3:

1) Courtship is depth. Dating is observation.
2) 1) Have the wisdom to evaluate the character of your partner
2) Have consistency in your dating relationship
3) Communicate
4) Have patience to let the relationship grow on God's time
3) Too much of a good thing can become a bore and make people dislike you.
4) As a couple goes deeper in a relationship, the woman comes out of "the clefts of the rock." They slowly discover one another.
5) God can forgive anything.

Application Answers Session 3

1) Women trying to change men after they are married. Trying to make them righteous men, when the whole time they dated he was not righteous.
2) You need to talk and tell each other how you feel and where you stand in the relationship.

Text Answers Session 4:

1) Resolve your problems as they occur.
2) God doesn't just create, He recreates. He can make it better.
3) *never borrow money in excess
   *never be unforgiving
   *don't have premarital sex
4) "You violate my daughter and may God curse your sex life."
5) I trust him. I belong to him. He is mine.

Application Answers Session 4:

5) My partner takes care of me. He/she never hurts me intentionally.
6) The man.

Text Answers Session 5:

1) 80, 60, 40, 1 out of 1051
2) They are strong in their character. They are consistent. They are godly men.
3) Her teeth are clean. Brush your teeth!
4) Don't get involved physically until you are married. Wait for God's time.
5) When a man is creative, passionate, ambitious and zealous at work, but placid, opinionless, uncommunicative, vacillating, not creative and a bad listener at home, the women in turn get mad.

Text Answers Session 6:

1) "A woman does not have authority over her own body, but the man does."
   *I Corinthians 7:4
2) Holy Spirit, Bible
3)   1) sex is gentle
            2) there are parameters that you and your mate will share
               when you make love
            3) sex is exhilarating
            4) sex is frightening
            5) sex is a means of union in a marriage
            6) sex is sensuous
            7) sex is holy
            8) sex is responsive
            9) sex is nourishing
            10) sex is pleasing to God
4) my
5) slow

Application Answers Session 6:

4) talk about sex

Text Answers Session 7:

1) 25%, 25%
2) Immaturity, character.
3) It is the average response of a pagan man. It's what everyone else does.
4) Like china or crystal, being fragile.
5) Holy Spirit.

Application Answers Session 7:

10) Teach, love, care and communicate
12) God is in control and not us. Leave it to Him to do the changing.

Text Answers Session 8:

1) It means his eyes don't ever change. They never narrow in anger.
2) You are gentle and unchanging in your love, just as Christ is.
3) *The man's mother
   *The woman's mother
   *sex
   *money
4) intimacy, joy.
5) When he took this woman and sat her in his chariot over the noble people, it meant "I not only forgive you, I can't even remember what you have done. It's like it never occurred."

Application Answers Session 8:

5) *the woman
   *the man

Text Answers Session 9:

1) A woman needs to be appreciated for her work.
2) 90%
3) God's plan is for marriage to get better and stronger with time, not worse.
4) Every woman has the desire to be "romanced."
5) In this culture, the belly was the heart of the emotions. Wheat was seen as the blessing of God. Solomon is saying that she is God's blessing to him.

Application Answers Session 9:

1)   1) The illusion fades
         2) Beauty fades
         3) You no longer remember; you take for granted your mate's faithfulness.
         4) Where after the sweetness fades, you are too lazy to discipline yourself to love and be committed to this person.
14 A) 1) You eliminate tenderness and respect.
         2) You meet someone.
         3) That person gives you the feelings your mate gave you, promised you and cut you off from.

4) You make sure you are in that person's presence, enjoying it from a distance. You fantasize about being with him/her.
5) You communicate to the person how you feel.
6) You have an affair.

B)   The E's are for ease

Text Answers Session 10:

1) Non-sexual touching
2) I revere you. I hold you with the utmost respect.
3) There were two pools at the gate of Rabbim. People would get into them for refreshment and for coolness.
4) The tower of Lebanon faced the enemy. As long as the tower was there, protecting the people, they knew they were safe. Her countenance is just as trusting as the tower.
5) Carmel was Israel's "postcard." It's where the great rolling hills were and the cattle would gather. His admiration deepened for her.

Application Answers Session 10:

1) You are a break for me to just be with you. You are a pleasure to me.
2) I can trust you.
3) You are the loveliest thing I know.
4) A) By a shellfish that came up on the land every so many years.
   B) Royalty

Text Answers Session 11:

1) Don't take the Lord's name in vain.
2) Cursing
   Not keeping your word
3) No human being can separate true devotion planned by God.
4) She is closed off to a man. She is moral. She is pure. She can say no.
5) 700%

Application Answers Session 11:

3) You were predetermined by God for each other.
   She gave you birth for your mate.
4)   A) I do not want any other woman in your heart and I don't want your
            arm around any other woman.
            B) Ownership
5)   A) Once you die you never come back. Love is as severe as death. It's
            permanent.
            B) Because it is a divine institution.
6) It is so permanent that it's the flame of God, because God's love is everlasting.
7) There's no flood that can make you give up/die on your love.
8) Hosea's wife left him to become a temple prostitute. He stayed faithful to God
   and continued to love her. This is a perfect example of how Christ loves us.
   (See the book of Hosea.)

Text Answers Session 12:

1) She found peace, knowing that God placed her in his path.
2) Daughters often get frustrated with fathers because they seem too protective.
   They are only doing the godly thing and taking care of their "fruit" (daughters).
3) To give yourself totally and completely to one another until the day you die.
4) Man cannot earn his way into the kingdom of Heaven. One must trust in Jesus
   Christ and believe He died on the cross so that we may have eternal life.
5)   1) Heaven is a free gift
            2) Man is a sinner
            3) God is Holy and must punish sin
            4) Jesus Christ is God's son. He lived the only perfect life for the
                   payment of sin
            5) Each person must respond to God with faith and trust in what Christ
               did on the Cross

Application Answers Session 12:

1) No. She wanted to run with her friends and thought her brothers were being
   too strict.
10) To place your mate in the arms of God.
13) Because I have trusted in Jesus Christ as my Lord and Savior. He died on the
   cross for my sins and because of that I am washed clean.
16) *Manianity: Man saves
   *Christianity: God saves through Jesus Christ.

Notes

Notes